## Drawing Legendary Monsters

# Drawing Dragons

## and Other Cold-Blooded Creatures

Steve Beaumont

PowerKiDS press

New York

Published in 2011 by The Rosen Publishing Group, Inc.
29 East 21st Street, New York, NY 10010

Artwork and text: Steve Beaumont and Dynamo Limited
Editors: Kate Overy and Joe Harris
U.S. Editor: Kara Murray
Designer: Steve Flight

Library of Congress Cataloging-in-Publication Data

Beaumont, Steve.
 Drawing dragons and other cold-blooded creatures / by Steve Beaumont.
    p. cm. — (Drawing legendary monsters)
 Includes index.
   ISBN 978-1-4488-3324-5 (library binding) — ISBN 978-1-4488-3257-6 (pbk.) — ISBN 978-1-4488-3258-3 (6-pack)
 1. Dragons in art—Juvenile literature. 2. Monsters in art-— Juvenile literature. 3. Drawing—Technique—Juvenile literature. I. Title.
 NC825.D72B43 2011
 743'.87—dc22

                                                  2010023191

Printed in China
SL001626US

CPSIA Compliance Information: Batch #WA11PK: For Further Information contact Rosen Publishing, New York, New York at 1-800-237-9932

# CONTENTS

# GETTING STARTED

**Before you can start creating fantastic artwork, you need some basic supplies. Take a look at this guide to help you get started.**

## PAPER

### Layout Paper
It's a good idea to buy inexpensive plain paper from a stationery shop for all of your practice work. Most professional illustrators use cheaper paper for basic layouts and practice sketches, before producing their final artworks on more costly paper.

### Heavy Drawing Paper
Heavy-duty, high-quality drawing paper is ideal for your final drawings. You don't have to buy the most expensive brand – most art or craft shops will stock their own brand or a student brand. Unless you're thinking of turning professional, these will do just fine.

### Watercolor Paper
This paper is made from 100 percent cotton, so it is much higher quality than wood-based paper. Most art shops stock a large range of weights and sizes. Using 140-pound (300 gsm) paper will be fine.

## PENCILS
Buy a variety of graphite (lead) pencils ranging from soft (#1) to hard (#4). Hard pencils last longer and leave less lead on the paper. Soft pencils leave more lead and wear down quickly. #2 pencils are a good medium option to start with. Spend time drawing with each pencil and get used to its qualities.

Another product to try is the mechanical pencil, in which you click the lead down the barrel using the button at the top. Try 0.5mm lead thickness to start with. These pencils are good for fine detail work.

### CIRCLE TEMPLATE
This is useful for drawing small circles.

### FRENCH CURVES
These are available in several shapes and sizes and are useful for drawing curves.

# INKING AND COLORING

**Once you have finished your pencil drawing, you need to add ink and color. Here are some tools you can use to get different results.**

## PENS

There are plenty of high-quality pens on the market these days that will do a decent job of inking. It's important to experiment with a range of different ones to decide with which ones you are comfortable working.

You may find you end up using a combination of pens to produce your finished artworks. Remember to use a pen with waterproof ink if you want to color your illustrations with a watercolor or ink wash. It's usually a good idea to use waterproof ink anyway as there's nothing worse than having your nicely inked drawing ruined by an accidental drop of water!

## PANTONE MARKERS

These are versatile, double-ended pens that give solid, bright colors. You can use them as you would regular marker pens or with a brush and a little water like a watercolor pen.

## BRUSHES

Some artists like to use a fine brush for inking linework. This takes a bit more practice and patience to master, but the results can be very satisfying. If you want to try your hand at brushwork, you should invest in some high-quality sable brushes.

## WATERCOLORS AND GOUACHE

Most art stores stock a wide range of these products, from professional to student quality.

# MASTER CLASS: SCALES AND SNAKES

## DRAWING SCALES

It's difficult to draw scales on a curved body. Here is a way that will make it easy for you to complete a detailed drawing. It's called the brick method.

**1**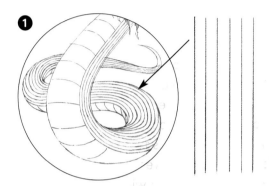

Start by drawing a series of vertical lines.

**2**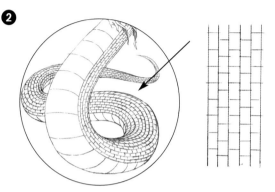

Next add staggered horizontal lines between the vertical lines, as if you were drawing a brick wall.

**3**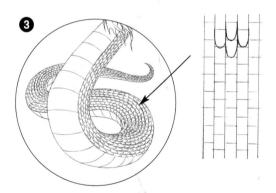

Round off the brick shapes to create the scales. Keep on doing this until you have a complete snake's skin.

**4**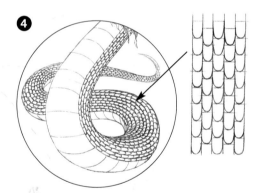

The final result is very realistic. Take a look at the basilisk on pages 14–19 for the full striking effect.

## SNAKE HEADS

When you come to the Medusa on pages 20–25, you will see that the snakes on her head are quite small. Here is a larger snake for you to study and copy.

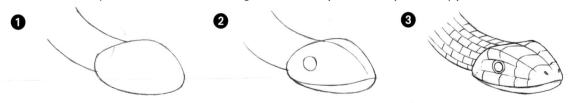

# MASTER CLASS: WING STRUCTURE

## DRAGON WINGS

A dragon's wings are similar to those of a bat. So it makes sense to base the construction of a dragon's wings on this small night-flying animal.

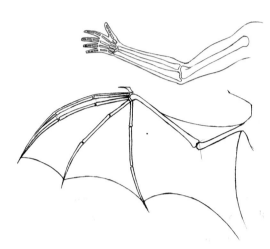

The structure of a bat's wing is similar to that of a human arm and hand. The bones of the wing form the shape of an arm and bend in the same places. The end of the wing is like a human hand, with four fingers and a short thumb. The difference is that a bat has a thin membrane stretching over this structure. You can break down drawing a bat's wing into the simple steps below.

**Picture 1** First plot out the wing. You need a short "thumb" at the top and four longer "fingers."

**Picture 2** Turn these lines into shapes by adding a second line close to the first line for each finger. Sketch the outline of the membrane.

**Picture 3** Now that you have the wing structure, highlight the bones by going over them with a thicker line.

**Picture 4** Clean up the drawing and add detail to the membrane to bring out the skin's texture.

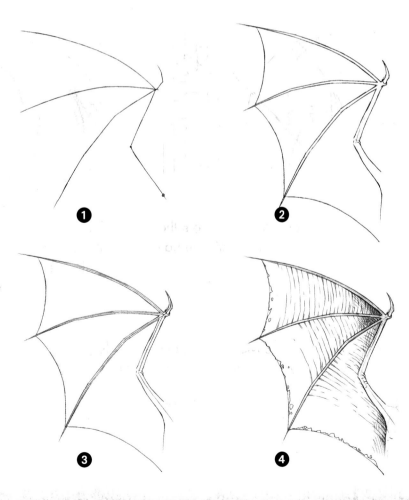

# DRAGON

A dragon, from the Greek word *drakon* meaning "serpent," is an enormous, frightening beast. Dragons live in underground dens filled with priceless, glittering treasures they have collected over centuries. Their huge wings and fiery breath make them terrifying adversaries.

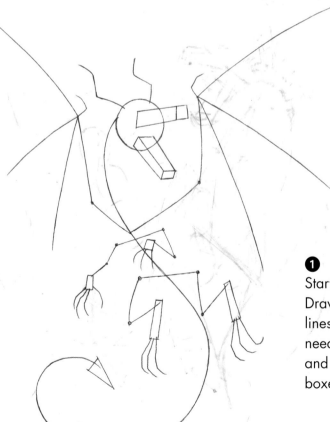

**1**
Start with the stick figure. Draw an S-shaped body and lines for the wings. You also need a circle for the head and two three-dimensional boxes for the mouth.

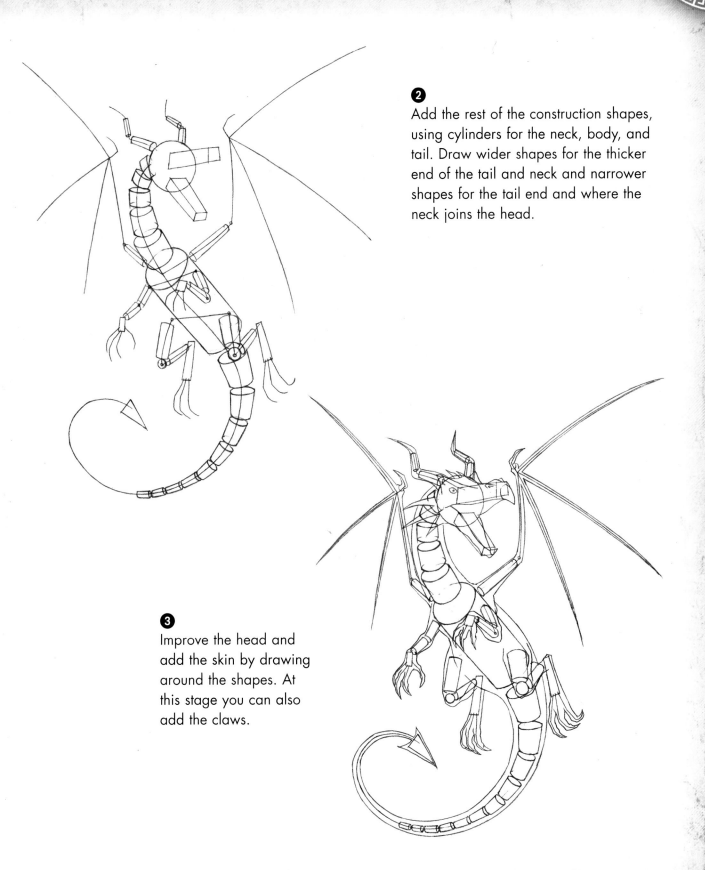

**2**

Add the rest of the construction shapes, using cylinders for the neck, body, and tail. Draw wider shapes for the thicker end of the tail and neck and narrower shapes for the tail end and where the neck joins the head.

**3**

Improve the head and add the skin by drawing around the shapes. At this stage you can also add the claws.

**4**
Develop the wings by drawing connection lines between the bone supports. Erase your construction shapes, then add detail to the underbelly. Make the teeth look uneven and irregular.

*Check out page 7 for tips on how to draw a dragon's wings.*

**❺**
Clean up the drawing and add detail to the skin and the wings. Try to create a torn, papery effect at the wing edges. Don't forget to include the fire coming out of the dragon's mouth.

**6**

Now that your pencil drawing is finished, you need to ink it over for a more dramatic effect.

# Dragon

**7**

Bring your dragon to life by adding color. Start by applying a beige base to the whole drawing.

Build up layers using a sandy color followed by gray on the belly and underside of the neck and wings.

For the upper body, use orange and dirty red. You can create dirty red by mixing red with a little gray.

# BASILISK

The title of king of the serpents belongs to the basilisk. Legend says it is the largest snake the world has ever known, although its ferocious head is birdlike rather than serpentine. Its breath is poisonous, but its greatest weapons are its piercing eyes: a single glance is fatal to anything it looks at.

**❶**
Start with an S shape to create the snake-like body. Include a circle for the head.

**2**

Draw the construction shapes using different-sized balls along the length of the body. Plot out the basilisk's beak with two triangles.

**3**

Create a smooth form over the shapes by adding the skin. Then draw the ferocious head. In mythology, the basilisk has the head of a cockerel, or a young rooster, with sharp teeth, demonic eyes, and a wild crest.

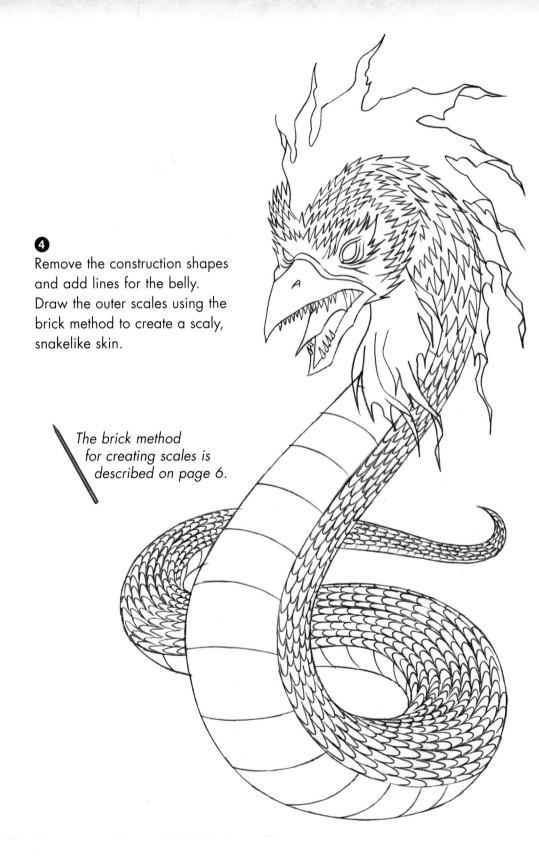

**❹**

Remove the construction shapes
and add lines for the belly.
Draw the outer scales using the
brick method to create a scaly,
snakelike skin.

*The brick method
for creating scales is
described on page 6.*

**TOP TIP**
*For light shading, draw fine slanted lines close together rather than shading in a solid block.*

**5** Complete the pencil drawing by adding detail to the head and body. Include light shading on the eyes, beak, and crest.

**6**

Now ink over the drawing. Keep the area around the eye dark to make it look scary and add heavier patches to the crest to give it depth.

# Basilisk

**7**

The final stage is to color your work.

Use a light gray base for the beak followed by buttercup yellow and rusty orange.

Color the underbelly with a beige base layer. Then add light gray.

Build up the colors on the crest with layers of orange and red. Use a midrange gray to create darker areas.

The scales have a warm red base followed by a darker red and dark gray for shading.

# MEDUSA

The Medusa's hair of squirming snakes marks her as a Gorgon, a type of Grecian reptile woman. Any living creature she looks at turns instantly to stone. However Medusa has a weakness, which is not shared by her sisters. Of all the Gorgons, she alone is mortal.

**1**

Begin with the stick figure. Draw the looping body carefully. Don't forget the hands.

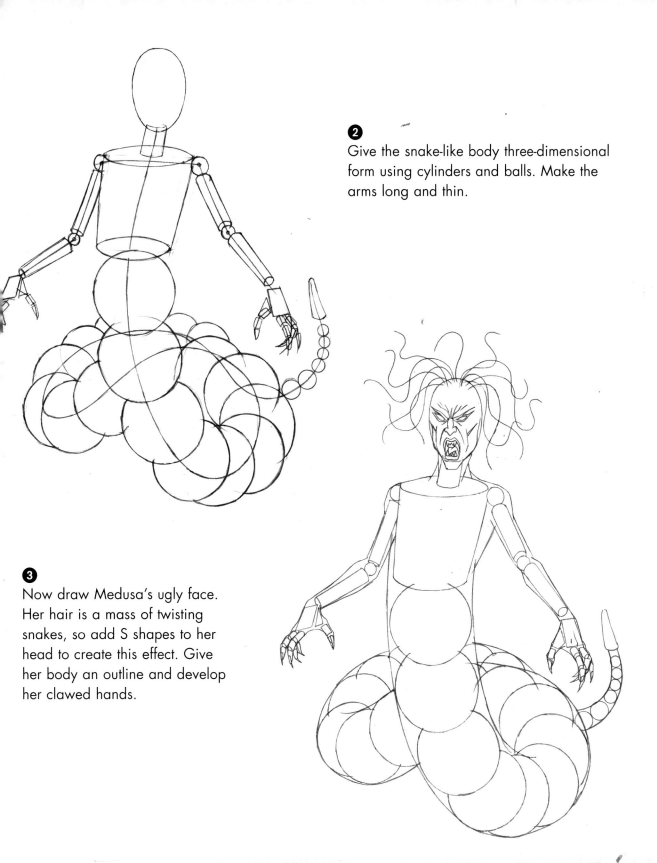

**2**

Give the snake-like body three-dimensional form using cylinders and balls. Make the arms long and thin.

**3**

Now draw Medusa's ugly face. Her hair is a mass of twisting snakes, so add S shapes to her head to create this effect. Give her body an outline and develop her clawed hands.

**4**

Remove the construction shapes, then draw the scales on the body. Add the necklace, other jewelry, and headdress. Improve Medusa's hair by giving the snakes an outline and drawing their heads.

*Find out how to draw snakes' heads close up on page 6.*

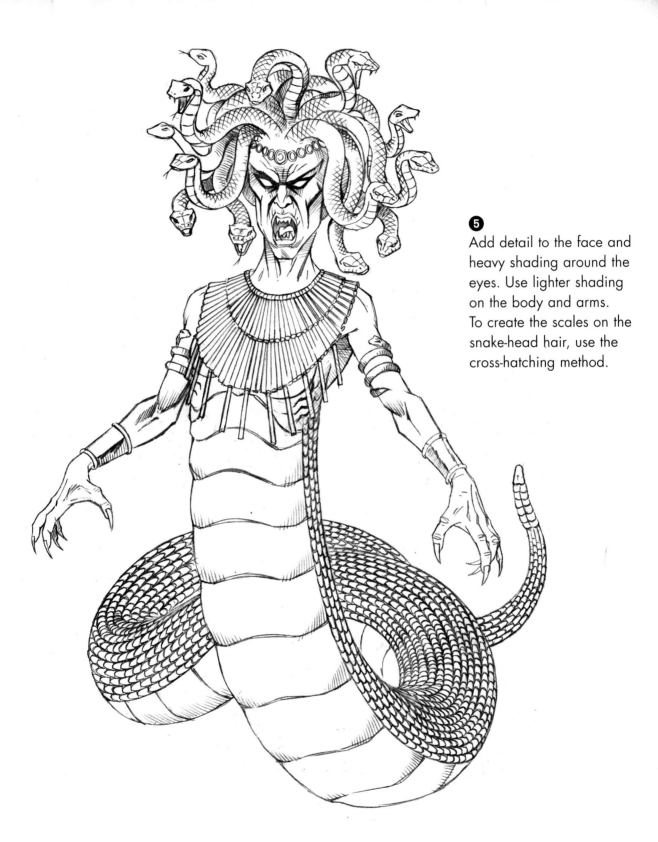

**5** Add detail to the face and heavy shading around the eyes. Use lighter shading on the body and arms. To create the scales on the snake-head hair, use the cross-hatching method.

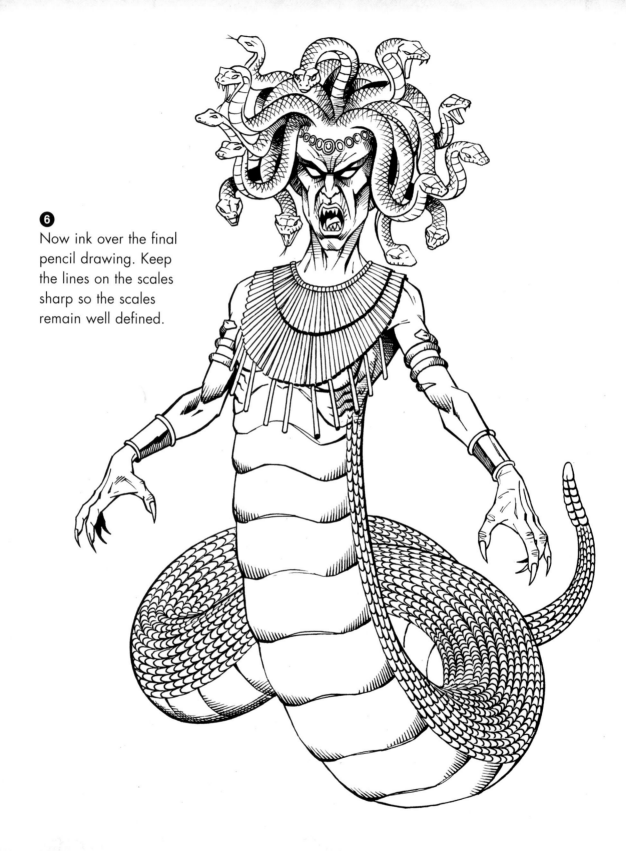

**6**
Now ink over the final
pencil drawing. Keep
the lines on the scales
sharp so the scales
remain well defined.

**7**
You can bring out
Medusa's fierceness and
snake-like qualities when
you color your art.

A pale skin tone
has been used
for the head and
arms followed
by layers of pale
green and gray.

Color the gold jewelry
with a yellow base. Add
yellow ochre and orange
to create darker tones.

The main body
has a pale olive
base of yellow
and gray.

The scales are grass green and emerald
green followed by dark green. You can
make green darker by adding dark gray.

# CREATING A SCENE: THE DRAGON'S CAVE

Many myths and legends tell of adventurers doing battle with dragons in caves deep beneath the earth. As they are suspicious, greedy creatures, dragons are drawn to underground hoards of precious metals. But woe betide anyone foolish enough to try to creep up on a sleeping dragon and snatch some treasure because these giant reptiles often sleep with one eye open!

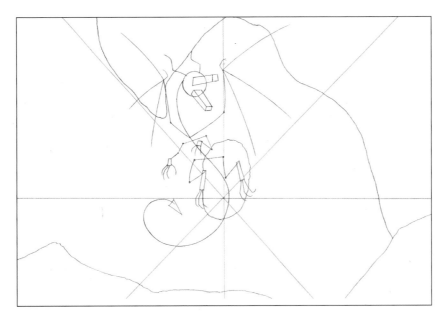

**1** Perspective is not absolutely required for this scene, as the action is set indoors. However you still need to add a vanishing point to give the effect that the dragon's cave continues deeper into the mountain. Note that the horizon is not exactly central. This adds height to the image.

**2** With the basic shape of the cave defined in your first lines, start to add more definition to the rock formations and stalactites. Not only does this flesh out detail, it also helps begin to build depth in your images.

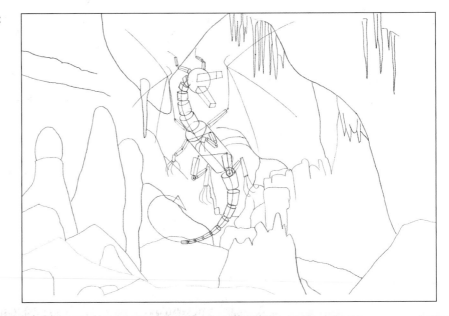

**3** Add more detail to the rock formations of the cave. Try to avoid uniformity in the layout of the lines to make a more natural-looking rock.

**4** Add shadow and texture to the rocks and gold hoard. Always bear in mind the direction of your light source, as this is important in making the image of the dragon and the background appear to be part of the same illustration.

**5** Shadow and texture play a very important part in the inking stage of this drawing. Keep your fill-ins light and build up gradually, as it is always easier to add depth of texture than it is to take it away. Ensure your lines on the rocky areas are kept sharp to maintain the idea of sharp and dangerous rocks.

**6** This dank and dingy underground cave has very little light coming in, although the treasure still glints brightly in the gloom. Use green and blue shades in the background to make it feel cold and unwelcoming. The addition of mossy tones suggests that it is an abandoned location in which a dragon would feel at home.

# GLOSSARY

**cross-hatching** (KRAWS-hach-ing)  A shading technique in which criss-crossing diagonal lines are overlapped to make an area of shadow.

**cylinder** (SIH-lin-der)  A shape with circular ends and straight sides.

**develop** (dih-VEH-lup)  To further or continue something.

**membrane** (MEM-brayn)  A thin sheet or skin that is part of a living organism.

**perspective** (per-SPEK-tiv)  Changing the size and shape of objects in a work of art to create a sense of nearness or distance.

**sketches** (SKECH-ez)  Quick drawings.

**texture** (TEKS-chur)  How something feels when you touch it.

**uniformity** (yoo-nuh-FAWR-muh-tee)  The quality of being consistently the same and unchanging.

**vanishing point** (VAN-ish-ing POYNT)  The point at which the lines showing perspective in a drawing meet each other.

**woe** (WOH)  Great sadness.

# INDEX

# WEB SITES

Due to the changing nature of internet links, PowerKids Press has developed an online list of Web sites related to the subject of this book. This site is updated regularly. Please use this link to access the list:
www.powerkidslinks.com/dlm/dragons/